sunday lunch

sunday lunch

British food for lazy days

This edition published in 2011
LOVE FOOD is an imprint of Parragon Books Ltd

Parragon
Queen Street House
4 Queen Street
Bath BA1 1HE, UK

ISBN: 978-1-4454-3795-8

Printed in China

Introduction by Linda Doeser

Notes for the Reader
This book uses both metric and imperial measurements. Follow the same units of measurement
throughout; do not mix metric ånd imperial. All spoon measurements are level: teaspoons are assumed
to be 5 ml, and tablespoons are assumed to be 15 ml. Unless otherwise stated, milk is assumed to be
full fat, eggs and individual vegetables are medium, and pepper is freshly ground black pepper.

The times given are an approximate guide only. Preparation times differ according to the techniques used
by different people and the cooking times may also vary from those given. Optional ingredients, variations
or serving suggestions have not been included in the calculations.

Recipes using raw or very lightly cooked eggs should be avoided by infants, the elderly, pregnant
women, convalescents and anyone suffering from an illness. Pregnant and breastfeeding women are
advised to avoid eating peanuts and peanut products. Sufferers from nut allergies should be aware that
some of the ready-made ingredients used in the recipes in this book may contain nuts. Always check the
packaging before use.

Contents

Sunday Lunch

In Isabella Beeton's famous nineteenth-century *Book of Household Management*, she devotes a section to seasonal menus to cover all contingencies from 'dinners for 18 persons' to 'kitchen dinners for 12 servants'. Among her recommendations for 'family dinners' on Sundays are (January) boned roast ribs of beef, potatoes, greens, horseradish sauce; (April) roast leg of mutton, broccoli, potatoes; (July) roast fillet of veal, bacon, peas, potatoes; and (October) roast goose, apple sauce, potatoes, cabbage. These dishes were all preceded by soup and followed by pudding, then fresh fruit and nuts. Even her 'little dinners', which she described as very economical, suggested such substantial fare as boned and stuffed loin of mutton, potatoes, mashed turnips; roast rib of beef, baked potatoes, greens; and boiled beef, carrots, potatoes, suet dumplings. These, too, were followed by pudding but soup was usually omitted.

Sunday dinner was, indeed, taken seriously then and for decades afterwards. Of course, at that time it was a very formal meal invariably eaten in the evening although, later, as society became less hidebound and in any case there were fewer – and eventually no – servants except in the wealthiest homes, this family feast tended to take place at lunchtime. Even in the second half of the last century, Sunday dinner was still a ritual that took place in homes all over Britain as families gathered to eat together, possibly for the first time in the week. A degree of formality still prevailed, as the table was laid with the best china and even a starched tablecloth and children were expected to mind their manners and not leave the table until everyone had finished.

In the past, Sunday was a much more special day of the week. Far more people attended church in the morning, with the children packed off to Sunday school; shops, cinemas and theatres were closed all day and pubs were open, if at all, only from noon until two o'clock. Also, until the post-war years, it was routine for offices to be open on Saturday mornings, so even those who didn't work shifts or in retail had only Sunday as a full day off. Probably the only person for whom it was not a 'day of rest' was the family cook.

Old England's roast beef

The beef of auld Scotland is worth a mention, too, as it is among the finest in the world, just as Welsh lamb has a unique sweetness and is meltingly tender. With such fine quality meat, it is hardly surprising that a roast became the traditional main course for dinner on this special day. It had other advantages too. It was ideal for feeding a large family and, quite often, guests as well. A 2.7-kg/6-lb boned and rolled rib of beef will easily feed ten people, though one can only imagine the size of the

family for whom Mrs Beeton recommended ribs in the plural. Any leftovers could be eaten cold or used to make another dish the following day.

Chicken was a latecomer to Sunday dinner as, for many years, birds were raised for their eggs rather than their meat. Unproductive tough old birds found their way into the pot, where they were stewed for several hours to render them edible – hardly a Sunday treat. As late as the 1950s roast chicken, although well suited to the smaller families of the mid-twentieth century, was still an expensive treat. Roast turkey had appeared on British tables earlier than chicken, replacing goose as the bird of choice because proportionately it provided far more meat.

As the Sunday roast grew ever more popular, traditional accompaniments and sauces also evolved. Roast potatoes were an obvious choice as they made economical use of the oven and could be cooked in the fat of the meat. This is a less popular idea in these health-conscious days, although there has been a huge increase in the purchase of goose fat for exactly this purpose. Even today, no one would dream of serving roast beef without Yorkshire pudding, although this used to be eaten with gravy before the expensive part of the meal, meat, was served in order to take the edge off the appetite. Poultry was served with bread sauce or cranberry sauce, while spicy horseradish and fruity apple sauces accompanied beef and pork respectively. Mint sauce, a peculiarly British concoction, is less popular than it once was and roast lamb is more likely to be served with redcurrant jelly, which also goes well with game and duck.

Contemporary options

About 100 years before Mrs Beeton no one would have been surprised to find fish on the Sunday menu. Wealthy Georgian families would sit down for Sunday dinner about four o'clock in the afternoon and a fish dish would often feature on the menu, although it must be said that they were a gluttonous bunch and many other dishes were included, too. Fish is a great choice for those who would prefer a lighter, more easily digestible meal than roast meat. A whole fish, such as salmon, can feed a family and guests – and, of course, it can be roasted too.

Options for vegetarians have, happily, moved on from the simulated meat dishes of lentils and nuts that would have been the only choice for a traditional-style Sunday dinner a few decades ago. Nowadays, the range of delicious and special vegetarian recipes will even tempt lovers of meat and two veg to try them.

Meat

Roast Beef & Yorkshire Pudding

Serves 8

- 3-kg/6 lb 8-oz joint of well-hung rib of beef on the bone
- olive oil
- salt and pepper

yorkshire pudding

- 250 g/9 oz plain flour, sifted
- 6 eggs
- ½ tsp salt
- 600 ml/1 pint milk

to serve

- roast potatoes (see page 70)
- gravy (see page 77)
- freshly cooked seasonal vegetables

1 To make the Yorkshire pudding, mix the flour, eggs and salt together in a bowl, then gradually add the milk as you stir with a whisk. When smooth set aside but don't chill.

2 Preheat the oven to 220°C/425°F/Gas Mark 7. Put a 40 x 25-cm/16 x 10-inch roasting tin in the bottom of the oven to warm for the Yorkshire puddings.

3 Rub a generous amount of olive oil and salt and pepper into the beef, then place in a roasting tin. Transfer to the preheated oven and roast for 30 minutes.

4 Reduce the temperature to 160°C/325°F/Gas Mark 3 and roast the beef for 60 minutes. Remove the beef from the oven and increase the temperature to 220°C/425°F/Gas Mark 7. Cover the beef with foil and leave to rest for at least 30 minutes.

5 Remove the roasting tin from the bottom of the oven and add the oil. Put it back in the oven for 5 minutes, then remove it and add the Yorkshire pudding batter. Put it back in the hot oven for about 20 minutes.

6 Remove the Yorkshire pudding from the oven. Cut the rib bones off the meat and carve the beef.

7 Serve with the Yorkshire pudding, roast potatoes, gravy and vegetables.

Beef Wellington

Serves 6

- 2 tbsp olive oil or vegetable oil
- 1.5 kg/3 lb 5 oz beef fillet, cut from the middle of the fillet, trimmed of fat and sinew
- 55 g/2 oz butter
- 150 g/5½ oz mushrooms, chopped
- 2 garlic cloves, crushed
- 150 g/5½ oz smooth liver pâté
- few drops of truffle oil (optional)
- 1 tbsp fresh parsley, finely chopped
- 2 tsp English mustard
- 500 g/1 lb 2 oz ready-made puff pastry
- 1 egg, lightly beaten
- salt and pepper

1 Place a large frying pan over a high heat and add the olive oil. Rub salt and pepper into the beef and sear all over very quickly in the pan. (This method gives a rare version. If you want it less rare, roast it at 220°C/425°F/Gas Mark 7 for 20 minutes at this stage.) Set aside to cool.

2 Heat the butter in a frying pan over a medium heat, add the mushrooms and fry for 5 minutes. Reduce the heat, add the garlic and fry for another 5 minutes. Put the mushrooms and garlic in a bowl, add the pâté, truffle oil, if using, and parsley, and beat with a fork. Leave to cool.

3 Rub the mustard into the seared beef fillet. Roll out the pastry into a rectangle large enough to wrap the whole fillet with some to spare. Spread the mushroom paste in the middle of the pastry in a shape the size of the base of the beef and lay the beef on top. Brush the edges of the pastry with beaten egg and fold it over, edges overlapping, and across the meat to enclose it completely.

4 Preheat the oven to 200°C/425°F/ Gas Mark 7. With the join underneath, place the wrapped beef in a roasting tin and brush with beaten egg. Leave to chill in the refrigerator for 15 minutes, then transfer to the preheated oven and bake for 50 minutes. Check after 30 minutes – if the pastry looks golden brown, cover it in foil to prevent it burning. Remove from the oven, cut into thick slices and serve.

Pot Roast with Potatoes & Dill

Serves 6

- 2½ tbsp plain flour
- 1 tsp salt
- ¼ tsp pepper
- 1 rolled brisket joint, weighing 1.6 kg/3 lb 8 oz
- 2 tbsp vegetable oil
- 2 tbsp butter
- 1 onion, finely chopped
- 2 celery sticks, diced
- 2 carrots, peeled and diced
- 1 tsp dill seed
- 1 tsp dried thyme or oregano
- 350 ml/12 fl oz red wine
- 150–225 ml/5–8 fl oz beef stock
- 4–5 potatoes, cut into large chunks and boiled until just tender
- 2 tbsp chopped fresh dill, to serve

1 Preheat the oven to 140°C/275°F/Gas Mark 1. Mix 2 tablespoons of the flour with the salt and pepper in a shallow dish. Dip the meat to coat. Heat the oil in a flameproof casserole and brown the meat all over. Transfer to a plate. Add half the butter to the casserole and cook the onion, celery, carrots, dill seed and thyme for 5 minutes. Return the meat and juices to the casserole.

2 Pour in the wine and enough stock to reach one third of the way up the meat. Bring to the boil, cover and cook in the oven for 3 hours, turning the meat every 30 minutes. After it has been cooking for 2 hours, add the potatoes and more stock if necessary.

3 When ready, transfer the meat and vegetables to a warmed serving dish. Strain the cooking liquid to remove any solids, then return the liquid to the casserole.

4 Mix the remaining butter and flour to a paste. Bring the cooking liquid to the boil. Whisk in small pieces of the flour and butter paste, whisking constantly until the sauce is smooth. Pour the sauce over the meat and vegetables. Sprinkle with the fresh dill to serve.

Rack of Lamb

Serves 4

- 2 x 4-rib racks of lamb, fat trimmed (but not removed) and bones trimmed of membrane
- olive oil
- 3 sprigs thyme
- large glass of Marsala, or white wine
- 2 tbsp water
- 1 tsp redcurrant jelly
- knob of butter
- salt and pepper
- Roast Potatoes (see page 70) and freshly cooked vegetables, to serve

1 Preheat the oven to 220°C/425°F/Gas Mark 7. Remove the lamb from the refrigerator. Lightly oil the racks all over, then rub salt and pepper into the fat and flesh using your fingers. Lay the two racks against each other in a roasting tin, ribs interlocking, skin on the outside. Slip the thyme in between the racks and wrap some foil around the bones at the end of the ribs to prevent them burning.

2 Place in the preheated oven and roast for 15 minutes, then reduce the oven temperature to 160°C/325°F/Gas Mark 3 and roast for a further 15 minutes (this will give you a nice, pink meat – if you prefer it well done, cook for 25 minutes). Remove from the oven and leave to rest (reserving the thyme and juices in the tin) while you make the gravy.

3 Pour off any excess fat from the roasting tin. If the thyme has burnt, discard and add another 2 sprigs, then add the Marsala, water and redcurrant jelly and stir. Place over a medium heat and simmer for 10 minutes until reduced by half. Stir in the butter.

4 Carve the lamb into individual chops and serve with the gravy, roast potatoes and vegetables.

Lamb Roasted with Lemon & Thyme

Serves 6

- 1 leg of lamb, 2.5–3 kg/5 lb 8 oz -6 lb 8 oz
- 250 ml/9 fl oz chicken stock
- 250 ml/9 fl oz red wine
- 1 tbsp redcurrant jelly
- seasonal vegetables and mint sauce, to serve

marinade

- 1 bulb of garlic, cloves separated but unpeeled
- 5 lemons or blood oranges
- 1 tbsp fresh rosemary leaves, chopped
- 1 tbsp fresh thyme leaves
- 2 tbsp salt

1 Remove the lamb from the refrigerator and pat dry with kitchen paper. Combine all the marinade ingredients in a food processor and blend to a paste.

2 Place the lamb in a roasting pan and cover with the paste so that it is completely encased. Cover loosely with foil and set aside in a cool place for an hour (or preferably in the refrigerator overnight). If the lamb has been in the refrigerator, remove it 30 minutes before cooking. Preheat the oven to 200°C/400°F/ Gas Mark 6. Put the foil-covered lamb into the oven and cook for 1¾ hours.

3 Remove from the oven and remove the lamb from the roasting pan. Reserve 2 tablespoons of the marinade paste, and let the lamb rest in the foil for 15–20 minutes.

4 Meanwhile, place the roasting tin over a medium–high heat, add the marinade paste, stock, wine and jelly and simmer until reduced by about half.

5 Carve the lamb, discarding most of the paste, and serve with the gravy, vegetables and mint sauce.

Roast Pork with Crackling

Serves 4

- 1 piece of loin of pork, weighing 1 kg/2 lb 4 oz, boned, and the rind removed and reserved
- 2 tbsp mustard
- salt and pepper
- apple sauce, to serve

1 Preheat the oven to 200°C/400°F/ Gas Mark 6.

2 Thoroughly score the pork with a sharp knife and sprinkle with salt. Place it on a wire rack on a baking tray and roast in the oven for 30–40 minutes until the crackling is golden brown and crisp.

3 Season the pork well with salt and pepper and spread the fat with the mustard. Place in a roasting tin and roast in the centre of the oven for 20 minutes. Reduce the oven temperature to 190°C/ 375°F/Gas Mark 5 and cook for a further 50–60 minutes until the meat is a good colour and the juices run clear when it is pierced with a skewer.

4 Remove the meat from the oven and place on a warmed serving plate, cover with foil and leave in a warm place.

5 Carve the pork into slices and serve on warmed plates with pieces of the crackling. Best served with apple sauce.

Roast Venison
with Brandy Sauce

Serves 4

- 6 tbsp vegetable oil
- 1.7 kg/3 lb 12 oz saddle of fresh venison, trimmed
- salt and pepper
- fresh thyme sprigs, to garnish
- roast potatoes (see page 70), to serve

brandy sauce

- 1 tbsp plain flour
- 4 tbsp vegetable stock
- 175 ml/6 fl oz brandy
- 100 ml/3½ fl oz double cream

1 Preheat the oven to 180°C/350°F/Gas Mark 4.

2 Heat half the oil in a frying pan over a high heat. Season the venison to taste with salt and pepper, add to the pan and cook until lightly browned all over. Pour the remaining oil into a roasting pan. Add the venison, cover with foil and roast in the oven, basting occasionally, for 1½ hours, or until cooked through. Remove from the oven and transfer to a warmed serving platter. Cover with foil and set aside.

3 To make the sauce, stir the flour into the roasting pan over the hob and cook for 1 minute. Pour in the stock and heat it, stirring to loosen the sediment from the base. Gradually stir in the brandy and bring to the boil, then reduce the heat and simmer, stirring, for 10–15 minutes until the sauce has thickened a little. Remove from the heat and stir in the cream.

4 Garnish the venison with thyme and serve with the brandy sauce and roast potatoes.

Veal & Sage Cutlets

Serves 8

- 8 small, thin veal cutlets, 70 g/2½ oz each
- 8 slices prosciutto
- 16 sage leaves
- flour for coating
- butter for frying
- 200 ml/7 fl oz dry white wine, plus extra for deglazing
- salt
- freshly ground pepper

1 Cover each cutlet with cling film and, using a rolling pin, flatten to a thickness of about 1 cm/½ in. Discard the cling film and season with salt and pepper. Place a slice of prosciutto and 2 sage leaves on each cutlet, fold over and secure with cocktail sticks. Lightly coat with flour on both sides and shake off any excess.

2 Heat the butter in a large frying pan. Cook the veal over a medium–high heat for about 2–3 minutes on each side, or until golden brown and cooked through.

3 Add the wine to the pan and continue to cook until thickened and reduced by half. Remove the cutlets from the pan and keep warm.

4 Deglaze the pan by pouring in the remaining wine over a medium heat. Stir and scrape up the browned bits from the bottom of the pan, using a wooden spatula, until the meat juices form a paste. Strain through a sieve and pour over the cutlets before serving.

Poultry

Roast Chicken

Serves 6

- 2.25 kg/5 lb free-range chicken
- 55 g/2 oz butter
- 2 tbsp chopped fresh lemon thyme
- 1 lemon, quartered
- 125 ml/4 fl oz white wine
- salt and pepper

1 Preheat the oven to 220°C/425°F/Gas Mark 7.

2 Make sure the chicken is clean, wiping it inside and out using kitchen paper, and place in a roasting tin.

3 In a bowl, soften the butter with a fork, mix in the lemon thyme and season well with salt and pepper.

4 Butter the chicken all over with the herb butter, inside and out, and place the lemon pieces inside the body cavity. Pour the wine over the chicken.

5 Roast in the centre of the oven for 20 minutes. Reduce the temperature to 190°C/375°F/Gas Mark 5 and continue to roast for a further $1\frac{1}{4}$ hours, basting frequently. Cover with foil if the skin begins to brown too much. If the tin dries out, add a little more wine or water.

6 Test that the chicken is cooked by piercing the thickest part of the leg with a sharp knife or skewer and making sure the juices run clear. Remove from the oven.

7 Remove the chicken from the roasting tin and place on a warm serving plate, cover with foil and leave to rest for 10 minutes before carving.

8 Place the roasting tin on the top of the stove and bubble the pan juices gently over a low heat until they have reduced and are thick and glossy. Season with salt and pepper to taste. Serve the chicken with the pan juices.

Roast Poussins

Serves 4

- 4 small poussins, weighing about 350–500 g/12 oz–1 lb 2 oz each
- 4 blades lemon grass
- 4 fresh kaffir lime leaves
- 4 slices fresh ginger
- about 6 tbsp coconut milk, for brushing
- freshly cooked basmati rice, to serve
- fresh coriander sprigs and lime wedges, to garnish

marinade

- 4 garlic cloves, peeled
- 2 fresh coriander sprigs
- 1 tbsp light soy sauce
- salt and pepper

1 Preheat the oven to 190°C/375°F/Gas Mark 5. Carefully wash the poussins and pat dry on kitchen paper.

2 Place all the ingredients for the marinade in a blender and purée until smooth. Alternatively, grind to a paste with a pestle and mortar.

3 Rub the marinade mixture into the skin of the poussins, using the back of a spoon to spread it evenly over the skins.

4 Place a blade of lemon grass, a lime leaf and a piece of ginger in the cavity of each poussin.

5 Place the poussins in a roasting tin and brush lightly with the coconut milk. Roast in the preheated oven for about 30 minutes.

6 Remove from the oven, brush again with coconut milk, then return to the oven and cook for a further 15–25 minutes, or until golden and cooked through, depending upon the size of the poussin. The poussins are cooked when the juices run clear when a skewer is inserted into the thickest part of the meat.

7 Serve the poussins with the pan juices poured over. Garnish with coriander sprigs and lime wedges and serve with freshly cooked basmati rice.

Traditional Roast Turkey

Serves 4

- 1 oven-ready turkey, weighing 5 kg/11 lb
- 1 garlic clove, finely chopped
- 100 ml/3½ fl oz red wine
- 70 g/2½ oz butter
- seasonal vegetables, to serve

stuffing

- 100 g/3½ oz button mushrooms
- 1 onion, chopped
- 1 garlic clove, chopped
- 85 g/3 oz butter
- 100 g/3½ oz fresh breadcrumbs
- 2 tbsp finely chopped fresh sage
- 1 tbsp lemon juice
- salt and pepper

port & cranberry sauce

- 100 g/3½ oz sugar
- 250 ml/9 fl oz port
- 175 g/6 oz fresh cranberries

1 Preheat the oven to 200°C/400°F/ Gas Mark 6.

2 To make the stuffing, clean and chop the mushrooms, put them in a saucepan with the onion, garlic and butter and cook for 3 minutes. Remove from the heat, stir in the remaining stuffing ingredients and season with salt and pepper. Rinse the turkey and pat dry with kitchen paper. Fill the neck end with stuffing and truss with string.

3 Put the turkey in a roasting tin. Rub the garlic over the bird and pour the wine over. Add the butter and roast in the oven for 30 minutes. Baste, then reduce the temperature to180°C/350°F/Gas Mark 4 and roast for a further 40 minutes. Baste again and cover with foil. Roast for a further 2 hours, basting regularly. Check that the bird is cooked by inserting a knife between the legs and body. If the juices run clear, it is cooked.

4 Remove from the oven, cover with foil and leave to stand for 25 minutes.

5 Meanwhile, put the sugar, port and cranberries in a saucepan. Heat over a medium heat until almost boiling. Reduce the heat, simmer for 15 minutes, stirring, then remove from the heat.

6 Carve the turkey and serve with the stuffing, port and cranberry sauce and seasonal vegetables.

Roast Turkey with Cider Sauce

Serves 8

- 1 boneless turkey breast roast, weighing 1 kg/2 lb 4 oz
- 1 tbsp sunflower or corn oil
- salt and pepper

stuffing
- 25 g/1 oz butter
- 2 shallots, finely chopped
- 1 celery stick, finely chopped
- 1 cooking apple, peeled, cored and diced
- 115 g/4 oz prunes, stoned and chopped
- 55 g/2 oz raisins
- 3 tbsp chicken stock
- 4 tbsp dry cider
- 1 tbsp chopped fresh parsley

cider sauce
- 1 shallot, very finely chopped
- 300 ml/10 fl oz dry cider
- 125 ml/4 fl oz chicken stock
- 1 tsp cider vinegar

1 Preheat the oven to 190°C/375°F/ Gas Mark 5.

2 To make the stuffing, melt the butter in a pan. Add the shallots and cook, for 5 minutes. Add the celery and apple and cook for 5 minutes. Add the remaining stuffing ingredients, cover, and simmer gently for 5 minutes, or until all the liquid has been absorbed. Transfer to a bowl and leave to cool.

3 Place the turkey roast on a cutting board and slice almost completely through, from the thin side toward the thicker side. Open out, place between 2 sheets of cling film, and flatten with a meat mallet to an even thickness. Season to taste with salt. Spoon on the cooled stuffing, roll the roast around it, and tie with kitchen string.

4 Heat the oil in a roasting pan over medium heat, add the roast, and brown all over. Transfer to the oven and roast for 1 hour 10 minutes, or until cooked through and the juices run clear when the meat is pierced with a skewer. Remove the roast from the pan and cover with foil.

5 To make the sauce, pour off any fat from the pan and set over medium heat. Add the shallot and half the cider and cook for 1–2 minutes, scraping any sediment from the bottom of the pan. Add the remaining cider, stock and vinegar and cook for 10 minutes, or until reduced and thickened. Remove and discard the string from the turkey and cut into slices. Serve with the cider sauce.

Roast Duck with Onion Marmalade

Serves 4

- 4 duck breasts, skin on, about 185 g/6½ oz each
- 2 tbsp runny honey
- salt and pepper
- freshly cooked vegetables, to serve

onion marmalade

- 50 g/1¾ oz butter
- 2 ripe but firm pears, peeled, cored and sliced
- 6 onions, sliced
- 2 tbsp dark chestnut honey
- 2 pieces stem ginger
- 2 tbsp stem ginger syrup

1 Preheat the oven to 200°C/400°F/ Gas Mark 6.

2 To make the marmalade, melt the butter in a saucepan over a medium–high heat, add the pears and onions and cook, stirring occasionally, for 10 minutes, or until soft and golden. Add the honey, stem ginger and ginger syrup and bubble gently for 15–20 minutes until the mixture is sticky and caramelized. Season to taste with salt and pepper. Keep warm until ready to serve, if necessary.

3 Meanwhile, heat a frying pan over a medium–high heat until hot. Add the duck breasts, skin-side down, to the hot frying pan. There is no need to add any fat; the breasts will release plenty as they cook. Cook for 2–3 minutes until golden brown. Turn the breasts over and cook for a further 2–3 minutes.

4 Transfer the breasts to a roasting dish, brush with the honey and season to taste with salt and pepper. Roast in the preheated oven for 12 minutes. Remove from the oven and leave to rest in a warm place for 5 minutes.

5 To serve, cut each duck breast into slices and fan out on each of four warmed dinner plates. Serve immediately with the onion marmalade and freshly cooked vegetables.

Roast Duck with Redcurrant Sauce

Serves 4

- 4 duck breasts, skin on, about 185 g/6½ oz each
- 4 shallots, finely chopped
- salt and pepper

redcurrant sauce

- 2 garlic cloves, crushed
- 2 tbsp fresh thyme leaves
- 200 ml/7 fl oz red wine
- 4 tbsp sherry or balsamic vinegar
- 85 g/3 oz redcurrant jelly
- 55 g/2 oz butter, cut into chunks

1 Preheat the oven to 180°C/350°F/ Gas Mark 4. Score the skin of each duck breast with four diagonal cuts down to the fat (but not into the meat). Season with salt and pepper. Place a large heavy-based frying pan over a high heat and add the duck breasts, skin-side down. There is no need to add any fat; the duck breasts will release plenty as they cook. Sear for about 10 minutes until the skin is crisp. Be careful, as they will spit. Turn the breasts over and sear on the other side for 2 minutes. Remove from the frying pan and put into a roasting tin. Keep warm.

2 Pour off most of the fat from the pan, reserving about a tablespoon. Put the pan over a medium heat, add the shallots and fry for 5–10 minutes until soft.

3 Meanwhile, put the duck breast into the preheated oven and cook for about 15 minutes (this will cook the duck to pink, which is how it ought to be served). Add the garlic and thyme to the pan and cook for a further 2 minutes. Add the wine and vinegar, simmer for 5 minutes, then stir in the redcurrant jelly and butter. When the duck is cooked, remove it from the oven, cover and keep warm for 5 minutes.

4 Cut each breast diagonally into five fat slices, lay on warmed plates and pour over the sauce.

Roast Pheasant with Red Wine & Herbs

Serves 4

- 100 g/3½ oz butter, slightly softened
- 1 tbsp chopped fresh thyme
- 1 tbsp chopped fresh parsley
- 2 oven-ready young pheasants
- 4 tbsp vegetable oil
- 125 ml/4 fl oz red wine
- salt and pepper

1 Preheat the oven to 190°C/375°F/ Gas Mark 5.

2 Put the butter in a small bowl and mix in the chopped herbs. Lift the skins off the pheasants, taking care not to tear them, and push the herb butter under the skins. Season to taste with salt and pepper. Pour the oil into a roasting tin, add the pheasants and cook in the oven for 45 minutes, basting occasionally.

3 Remove from the oven, pour over the wine, then return to the oven and cook for a further 15 minutes, or until cooked through. Check that each bird is cooked by inserting a knife between the legs and body. If the juices run clear, they are cooked.

4 Remove the pheasants from the oven, cover with foil and leave to stand for 15 minutes. Carve the pheasants and serve.

Roast Goose with Apple Stuffing

Serves 8

- 1 goose with giblets, about 4.5 kg/10 lb
- salt

apple stuffing

- 55 g/2 oz butter
- 2 large onions, finely chopped
- 200 g/7 oz celery, finely chopped
- 2 Bramley apples, peeled, cored and chopped
- 200 g/7 oz carrots, grated
- 200 g/7 oz fresh breadcrumbs
- 1 tbsp chopped fresh sage
- 150 ml/5 fl oz white wine

1 Remove the giblets from the bird and wipe it thoroughly inside with kitchen paper. Chop the liver and reserve for the stuffing.

2 Place a large saucepan over a medium heat and add the butter. When the butter is melted add the onion, celery and apples and slowly fry for about 20 minutes, until soft. Add the liver, carrots, breadcrumbs, sage and wine and cook gently for a further 15 minutes.

3 Preheat the oven to 220°C/425°F/Gas Mark 7. Fill the main cavity of the bird with the stuffing and put any excess in an ovenproof bowl to cook alongside the goose. Rub the goose all over with salt and place it on a rack above a roasting tin. Roast for 30 minutes, then reduce the oven temperature to 180°C/350°F/Gas Mark 4 and continue to roast for a further 1½–2 hours (the bird is cooked when the juices run clear when the thigh is pricked with a skewer). Remove from the oven, cover, and leave to rest for 20 minutes.

4 Scoop out the stuffing, carve the goose and serve.

Fish & Vegetables

Classic Fish Pie

Serves 6-8

- 1 kg/2 lb 4 oz floury potatoes, such as Maris Piper or Desiree
- 150 g/5½ oz butter, plus extra for greasing
- 500 ml/18 fl oz milk
- 600 g/1 lb 5 oz firm white fish fillets, such as cod, haddock or pollack
- 400 g/14 oz undyed smoked haddock fillet
- 3 bay leaves
- 55 g/2 oz plain flour
- handful of fresh parsley, chopped
- 250 g/9 oz cooked peeled prawns
- 4 hard-boiled eggs, shelled and quartered
- 55 g/2 oz melted butter
- salt and pepper

1 Peel and quarter the potatoes. Bring a large saucepan of lightly salted water to the boil, add the potatoes and cook for 15–20 minutes, or until tender. Drain, mash thoroughly with half of the butter and 2 tablespoons of the milk, then season with salt and pepper, cover and keep warm.

2 Preheat the oven to 200°C/400°F/Gas Mark 6. Place the fish fillets in a shallow saucepan and pour over the remaining milk. Add the bay leaves and place over a low heat. Bring the milk to a gentle simmer and poach the fish for 4 minutes (it shouldn't be fully cooked as it will be baked later). Remove from the saucepan and place on a plate, discard the bay leaves and reserve the milk. Remove any remaining bones and skin from the fish and flake into large chunks. Put in a bowl, cover and set aside.

3 Melt the remaining butter in a saucepan, then stir in the flour to make a roux and cook, stirring occasionally, for 3 minutes. Gradually add the reserved milk, a ladleful at a time, and mix into the roux. Add the parsley, the cooked fish, the prawns and the eggs. Fold carefully together. Season to taste with salt and pepper.

4 Butter a pie dish and fill it with the fish mixture. Lay the potatoes on top, making a pattern. Drip the melted butter over the whole pie, place in the preheated oven and bake for 30–40 minutes until the top is golden brown.

Garlic-crusted Roast Haddock

Serves 4

- 900 g/2 lb floury potatoes
- 125 ml/4 fl oz milk
- 55 g/2 oz butter
- 4 haddock fillets, about 225 g/8 oz each
- 1 tbsp sunflower oil
- 4 garlic cloves, finely chopped
- salt and pepper
- 2 tbsp chopped fresh parsley, to garnish

1 Preheat the oven to 230°C/450°F/Gas Mark 8.

2 Cut the potatoes into chunks and cook in a saucepan of lightly salted water for 15 minutes, or until tender. Drain well. Mash in the saucepan until smooth. Set over a low heat and beat in the milk, butter and salt and pepper to taste.

3 Put the haddock fillets in a roasting tin and brush the fish with the oil. Sprinkle the garlic on top, add salt and pepper to taste, then spread with the mashed potatoes. Roast in the oven for 8–10 minutes, or until the fish is just tender.

4 Meanwhile, preheat the grill. Transfer the fish to the grill and cook for about 2 minutes, or until golden brown. Sprinkle with the chopped parsley and serve immediately.

Roast Salmon with Lemon & Herbs

Serves 4

- 6 tbsp extra virgin olive oil
- 1 onion, sliced
- 1 leek, trimmed and sliced
- juice of ½ lemon
- 2 tbsp chopped fresh parsley
- 2 tbsp chopped fresh dill
- 500 g/1 lb 2 oz salmon fillets
- salt and pepper
- freshly cooked baby spinach leaves and lemon wedges, to serve

1 Preheat the oven to 200°C/400°F/Gas Mark 6. Heat 1 tablespoon of the oil in a frying pan over a medium heat. Add the onion and leek and cook, stirring, for about 4 minutes until slightly soft.

2 Meanwhile, put the remaining oil in a small bowl with the lemon juice and herbs, and season. Stir together well. Rinse the fish under cold running water, then pat dry with kitchen paper. Arrange the fish in a shallow, ovenproof baking dish.

3 Remove the frying pan from the heat and spread the onion and leek over the fish. Pour the oil mixture over the top, ensuring that everything is well coated. Roast in the centre of the preheated oven for about 10 minutes or until the fish is cooked through.

4 Arrange the cooked spinach on warmed serving plates. Remove the fish and vegetables from the oven and arrange on top of the spinach. Serve immediately with lemon wedges.

Roast Sea Bass

Serves 4

- 1.3–1.8 kg/3–4 lb whole sea bass, gutted
- 1 small onion, finely chopped
- 2 garlic cloves, finely chopped
- 2 tbsp finely chopped fresh herbs, such as parsley, chervil and tarragon
- 25 g/1 oz anchovy fillets, finely chopped
- 25 g/1 oz butter
- 150 ml/5 fl oz white wine
- 2 tbsp crème fraîche
- salt and pepper

1 Preheat the oven to 200°C/400°F/Gas Mark 6.

2 Remove any scales from the fish and clean it thoroughly both inside and out. If desired, trim off the fins with a pair of scissors. Using a sharp knife, make five or six cuts diagonally into the flesh of the fish on both sides. Season well with salt and pepper, both inside and out.

3 Mix the onion, garlic, herbs and anchovies together in a bowl.

4 Stuff the fish with half the mixture and spoon the remainder into a roasting tin. Place the sea bass on top.

5 Spread the butter over the sea bass, pour over the wine and place in the oven. Roast for 30–35 minutes until the fish is cooked through.

6 Remove the fish from the tin to a warmed serving dish. Return the tin to the top of the stove and stir the onion mixture and juices together over a medium heat. Add the crème fraîche and pour into a warmed serving bowl.

7 Serve the sea bass whole and divide at the table. Spoon a little sauce on the side.

Nutty Stilton Roast

Serves 6-8

- 2 tbsp virgin olive oil, plus extra for oiling
- 2 onions, one finely chopped and one cut into thin wedges
- 3–5 garlic cloves, crushed
- 2 celery stalks, finely sliced
- 175 g/6 oz cooked and peeled chestnuts
- 175 g/6 oz mixed chopped nuts
- 55 g/2 oz ground almonds
- 55 g/2 oz fresh wholemeal breadcrumbs
- 225 g/8 oz Stilton cheese, crumbled
- 1 tbsp chopped fresh basil
- 1 egg, beaten
- 1 red pepper, peeled, deseeded and cut into thin wedges
- 1 courgette, about 115 g/4 oz, cut into wedges
- salt and pepper

1 Preheat the oven to 180°C/350°F/ Gas Mark 4. Lightly grease a 900-g/ 2-lb loaf tin. Heat 1 tablespoon of the oil in a frying pan over medium heat, add the chopped onion, 1–2 of the garlic cloves, and the celery and cook for 5 minutes, stirring occasionally.

2 Remove from the pan, drain through a sieve and transfer to a food processor with the nuts, breadcrumbs, half the cheese and the basil. Using the pulse button, blend the ingredients together, then slowly blend in the egg to form a stiff mixture. Season.

3 Heat the remaining oil in a frying pan over medium heat, add the onion wedges, remaining garlic, red pepper and courgette and cook for 5 minutes, stirring frequently. Remove from the pan, add salt and pepper and drain through a sieve.

4 Place half the nut mixture in the prepared tin and smooth the surface. Cover with the onion and red pepper mixture and crumble over the remaining cheese. Top with the remaining nut mixture and press down firmly. Cover with foil. Bake in the preheated oven, for 45 minutes. Remove the foil and bake for a further 25–35 minutes, or until cooked and firm to the touch.

5 Remove from the oven, cool in the pan for 5 minutes, then turn out and serve.

Asparagus & Tomato Tart

Serves 4

- 375 g/13 oz ready-made shortcrust pastry
- butter, for greasing
- 1 bunch thin asparagus spears
- 250 g/9 oz spinach leaves
- 3 large eggs, beaten
- 150 ml/5 fl oz double cream
- 1 garlic clove, crushed
- 10 small cherry tomatoes, halved
- handful of fresh basil, chopped
- 25 g/1 oz grated Parmesan cheese
- salt and pepper

1 Preheat the oven to 190°C/375°F/ Gas Mark 5. Grease a 25–30-cm/10–12-inch tart tin. Remove the pastry from the refrigerator at least 15 minutes before use, otherwise it may be brittle and difficult to handle. Roll out the pastry and use to line the prepared tin. Cut off any excess, prick the base with a fork, cover with a piece of greaseproof paper and fill with baking beans, then bake blind for 20–30 minutes until lightly browned.

2 Remove from the oven and leave to cool slightly. Reduce the oven temperature to 180°C/350°F/Gas Mark 4.

3 Meanwhile, bend the asparagus spears until they snap, and discard the woody bases. Bring a large saucepan of water to the boil, add the asparagus and blanch for 1 minute, then remove and drain. Add the spinach to the boiling water, then remove immediately and drain very well.

4 Mix the eggs, cream and garlic together and season with salt and pepper. Lay the blanched spinach at the bottom of the pastry base, add the asparagus and tomatoes, cut side up, in any arrangement you like, scatter over the basil, then pour the egg mixture on top. Transfer to the oven and bake for about 35 minutes, or until the filling has set nicely. Sprinkle the Parmesan cheese on top and leave to cool to room temperature before serving.

Squash, Sage & Gorgonzola Tart

Serves 6

pastry

- 75 g/2¾ oz cold butter, cut into pieces, plus extra for greasing
- 125 g/4½ oz plain flour
- pinch of salt
- cold water

filling

- ½ small butternut squash or 1 slice pumpkin, weighing 250 g/9 oz
- 1 tsp olive oil
- 250 ml/9 fl oz double cream
- 175 g/6 oz Gorgonzola cheese
- 2 eggs, plus 1 egg yolk
- 6–8 fresh sage leaves
- salt and pepper

1 Cut the squash in half and brush the cut side with the oil. Place cut-side up on a baking tray and bake for 30–40 minutes, until browned and very soft. Leave to cool. Remove the seeds and scoop out the flesh into a large bowl, discarding the skin.

2 To make the pastry, lightly grease a 22 cm/8½ in loose-bottomed fluted tart tin. Sift the flour and salt into a food processor, add the butter and process until the mixture resembles fine breadcrumbs. Tip the mixture into a large bowl and add a little cold water, just enough to bring the dough together. Turn out on to a floured surface and roll out the pastry 8 cm/3¼ inches larger than the tin. Carefully lift the pastry into the tin and press to fit. Roll the rolling pin over the tin to neaten the edges and remove the excess pastry from the edges. Fit a piece of baking paper into the tart case, fill with baking beans and chill in the refrigerator for 30 minutes. Meanwhile, preheat the oven to 190°C/375°F/ Gas Mark 5.

3 Remove the pastry case from the refrigerator and bake the tart case blind for 10 minutes in the preheated oven then remove the beans and paper. Return to the oven for 5 minutes.

4 Mash the squash and mix with half the cream, season with salt and pepper and spread in the pastry case. Slice the cheese and lay it on top. Whisk the remaining cream with the eggs and egg yolk and pour the mixture into the tart tin, making sure it settles evenly. Arrange the sage leaves in a circle on the surface. Bake for 30–35 minutes and leave for 10 minutes in the tin before serving.

Roast Butternut Squash

Serves 4

- 1 butternut squash, about 450 g/1 lb
- 1 onion, chopped
- 2–3 garlic cloves, crushed
- 4 small tomatoes, chopped
- 85 g/3 oz chestnut mushrooms, chopped
- 85 g/3 oz canned butter beans, drained, rinsed and roughly chopped
- 1 courgette, about 115 g/4 oz, trimmed and grated
- 1 tbsp chopped fresh oregano, plus extra to garnish
- 2 tbsp tomato purée
- 300 ml/10 fl oz water
- 4 spring onions, trimmed and chopped
- 1 tbsp Worcestershire sauce, or to taste
- pepper

1 Preheat the oven to 190°C/375°F/Gas Mark 5. Prick the squash all over with a metal skewer then roast for 40 minutes, or until tender. Remove from the oven and leave until cool enough to handle.

2 Cut the squash in half, scoop out and discard the seeds then scoop out some of the flesh, making hollows in both halves. Chop the scooped out flesh and put in a bowl. Place the two halves side by side in a large roasting tin.

3 Add the onion, garlic, chopped tomatoes and mushrooms to the squash flesh in the bowl. Add the roughly chopped butter beans, grated courgette, chopped oregano and pepper to taste and mix well. Spoon the filling into the 2 halves of the squash, packing it down as firmly as possible.

4 Mix the tomato purée with the water, spring onions and Worcestershire sauce in a small bowl and pour around the squash.

5 Cover loosely with a large sheet of foil and bake for 30 minutes, or until piping hot. Serve in warmed bowls, garnished with chopped oregano.

Sides & Accompaniments

Brussels Sprouts with Buttered Chestnuts

Serves 4

- 350 g/12 oz Brussels sprouts, trimmed
- 3 tbsp butter
- 100 g/3½ oz canned whole chestnuts
- pinch of nutmeg
- salt and pepper
- 50 g/1¾ oz flaked almonds, to garnish

1 Bring a large saucepan of lightly salted water to the boil. Add the Brussels sprouts, bring back to the boil and cook for 5 minutes. Drain thoroughly.

2 Melt the butter in a large saucepan over a medium heat. Add the Brussels sprouts and cook, stirring, for 3 minutes, then add the chestnuts and nutmeg.

3 Season with salt and pepper and stir well. Cook for another 2 minutes, stirring, then remove from the heat. Transfer to a serving dish, scatter over the almonds and serve.

Glazed Turnips

Serves 4-6

- 900 g/2 lb young turnips, peeled and quartered
- 55 g/2 oz butter
- 1 tbsp brown sugar
- 150 ml/5 fl oz vegetable stock
- 1 sprig of fresh rosemary
- salt and pepper

1 Put the turnip into a saucepan of boiling salted water, bring back to the boil and simmer for 10 minutes. Drain well.

2 Melt the butter in the rinsed-out saucepan over a gentle heat, add the turnip and sugar and mix to coat well.

3 Add the stock with the rosemary and bring to the boil. Reduce the heat and simmer for 15–20 minutes with the lid off the pan so that the juices reduce and the turnips are tender and well glazed.

4 Remove the pan from the heat, discard the rosemary and season with salt and pepper to taste.

5 Serve immediately with roast lamb, pork, or duck.

Honey-glazed Red Cabbage with Sultanas

Serves 4

- 2 tbsp butter
- 1 garlic clove, chopped
- 650 g/1 lb 7 oz red cabbage, shredded
- 150 g/5½ oz sultanas
- 1 tbsp honey
- 100 ml/3½ fl oz red wine
- 100 ml/3½ fl oz water

1 Melt the butter in a large saucepan over a medium heat. Add the garlic and cook, stirring, for 1 minute, until slightly softened.

2 Add the cabbage and sultanas, then stir in the honey. Cook for another minute. Pour in the wine and water and bring to the boil. Reduce the heat, cover and simmer, stirring occasionally, for about 45 minutes or until the cabbage is cooked. Serve hot.

Perfect Roast Potatoes

Serves 6

- 1.3 kg/3 lb large floury potatoes, such as King Edwards, Maris Piper or Desiree, peeled and cut into even-sized chunks
- 3 tbsp dripping, goose fat, duck fat or olive oil
- salt

1 Preheat the oven to 220°C/425°F/ Gas Mark 7.

2 Cook the potatoes in a large saucepan of boiling salted water over a medium heat, covered, for 5–7 minutes. They will still be firm. Remove from the heat.

3 Meanwhile, add the fat to a roasting tin and place in the hot oven.

4 Drain the potatoes well and return them to the saucepan. Cover with the lid and firmly shake the pan so that the surface of the potatoes is roughened to help give a much crisper texture.

5 Remove the roasting tin from the oven and carefully tip the potatoes into the hot oil. Baste them to ensure they are all coated with the oil.

6 Roast at the top of the oven for 45–50 minutes until they are browned all over and thoroughly crisp. Turn the potatoes and baste again only once during the process or the crunchy edges will be destroyed.

7 Carefully transfer the potatoes from the roasting tin into a warmed serving dish. Sprinkle with a little salt and serve at once.

Mashed Potatoes

Serves 4

- 900 g/2 lb floury potatoes, such as King Edwards, Maris Piper or Desirée
- 55 g/2 oz butter
- 3 tbsp hot milk
- salt and pepper

1 Peel the potatoes, placing them in cold water as you prepare the others to prevent them from going brown.

2 Cut the potatoes into even-sized chunks and cook in a large saucepan of boiling salted water over a medium heat, covered, for 20–25 minutes until they are tender. Test with the point of a knife, but do make sure you test right to the middle to avoid lumps.

3 Remove the pan from the heat and drain the potatoes. Return the potatoes to the hot pan and mash with a potato masher until smooth.

4 Add the butter and continue to mash until it is all mixed in, then add the milk (it is better hot because the potatoes absorb it more quickly to produce a creamier mash).

5 Taste the mash and season with salt and pepper as necessary. Serve immediately.

Bread Sauce

Serves 6-9

- 1 onion
- 12 cloves
- 1 bay leaf
- 6 black peppercorns
- 600 ml/1 pint milk
- 115 g/4 oz fresh white breadcrumbs
- 2 tbsp butter
- whole nutmeg, for grating
- 2 tbsp double cream (optional)
- salt and pepper

1 Make small holes in the onion using the point of a sharp knife or a skewer, and stick the cloves in them.

2 Put the onion, bay leaf and peppercorns in a saucepan and pour in the milk. Bring to the boil, then remove from the heat, cover and leave to infuse for 1 hour.

3 To make the sauce, discard the onion and bay leaf and strain the milk to remove the peppercorns. Return the milk to the cleaned pan and add the breadcrumbs.

4 Cook the sauce over a very low heat for 4–5 minutes, until the breadcrumbs have swollen and the sauce is thick.

5 Beat in the butter and season well with salt and pepper and a good grating of nutmeg. Stir in the cream just before serving, if using.

Horseradish Sauce

Serves 6-8

- 6 tbsp creamed horseradish sauce
- 6 tbsp crème fraîche

1 In a small serving bowl, mix the horseradish sauce and crème fraîche together. Serve the sauce with roast beef, or with smoked fish such as trout or mackerel.

Cranberry Sauce

makes about 450 ml/16 fl oz

- 450 g/1 lb fresh or thawed frozen cranberries
- 1 tbsp grated orange rind, preferably unwaxed
- 150 ml/5 fl oz freshly squeezed orange juice
- 115 g/4 oz soft light brown sugar
- 150 ml/5 fl oz water
- 1–2 tbsp Cointreau (optional)

1 Put the cranberries in a heavy-based saucepan with the orange rind and juice, most of the sugar and the water. Bring to the boil, then reduce the heat and simmer for 12–15 minutes until the cranberries have burst.

2 Remove from the heat, taste and add the remaining sugar, if liked, with the Cointreau, if using. Serve warm or cold.

Gravy

makes about 1.2 litres/2 pints

- 2 tbsp plain flour
- 1 litre/1¾ pints stock
- 125 ml/4 fl oz red wine or sherry
- salt and pepper

1 Place a roasting tin with any remaining meat sediment over a low heat on top of the stove.

2 Sprinkle in the flour, stir well using a small whisk to make a smooth paste and cook for 1 minute. Add the stock a little at a time, whisking constantly, until you have a smooth gravy.

3 Add the wine and bubble together until the gravy is slightly reduced. Season to taste with salt and pepper.

4 When you carve the meat, some juices will escape: add these to the gravy and stir. Carefully pour the gravy into a warm serving jug and serve.

Chestnut & Sausage Stuffing

Serves 6-8

- 225 g/8 oz pork sausage meat
- 225 g/8 oz unsweetened chestnut purée
- 85 g/3 oz walnuts, chopped
- 115 g/4 oz ready-to-eat dried apricots, chopped
- 2 tbsp chopped fresh parsley
- 2 tbsp snipped fresh chives
- 2 tsp chopped fresh sage
- 4–5 tbsp double cream
- salt and pepper

1 Preheat the oven to 190°C/375°F/ Gas Mark 5. Combine the sausage meat and chestnut purée in a bowl, then stir in the walnuts, apricots, parsley, chives and sage. Stir in enough cream to make a firm, but not dry, mixture. Season to taste with salt and pepper.

2 If you are planning to stuff a turkey or goose, fill the neck cavity only to ensure the bird cooks all the way through. It is safer and more reliable to cook the stuffing separately, either rolled into small balls and placed on a baking sheet or spooned into an ovenproof dish.

3 Cook the separate stuffing in a preheated oven for 30–40 minutes at 190°C/375°F/Gas Mark 5. It should be allowed a longer time to cook if you are roasting a bird at a lower temperature in the same oven.